Further Lovely Lettuce Lore

(from Anna's salad days)

poems by

Julie Cooper-Fratrik

Finishing Line Press
Georgetown, Kentucky

Further Lovely Lettuce Lore

(from Anna's salad days)

for Nura,
my Anna

Copyright © 2018 by Julie Cooper-Fratrik
ISBN 978-1-63534-375-5 First Edition
All rights reserved under International and Pan-American Copyright Conventions.
No part of this book may be reproduced in any manner whatsoever without written permission from the publisher, except in the case of brief quotations embodied in critical articles and reviews.

ACKNOWLEDGMENTS

Grateful acknowledgment to the publishers of the publications in which these poems first appeared:

"Near dusk..." was published as part of "Dinner Party," *Art Times*;
"In the Morning, What the Light Provides" was published as part of "Bodies in Intercourse: Within the Jouisspace" (Chapter Five of *Beyond the Objects of Desire: The Space of the Poet in the Space of the World*) in *Under the Sun*;
In "Anna's Reveries," "where have you come from..." was published under a different title in *The Comstock Review*;
"Anna Counts the Morning Blackbirds" was published in slightly different form in *The Styles*;
"Digression: Sad Young Man on a Train" was published as "Three Stories, Only Two of Which are for Grownups" in *Natural Bridge*;
Sections of "Anna's House," sometimes in different form, have been published in *So To Speak, Last Tangos, Art Times*, and *Making Our Own Light: An Anthology* (The Bucks County Poet Laureate Program).

Publisher: Leah Maines

Editor: Christen Kincaid

Cover Art: Nura Petrov

Cover Design: Elizabeth Maines McCleavy

Printed in the USA on acid-free paper.
Order online: www.finishinglinepress.com
also available on amazon.com

Author inquiries and mail orders:
Finishing Line Press
P. O. Box 1626
Georgetown, Kentucky 40324
U. S. A.

Table of Contents

In the Morning, What the Light Provides 1

Anna's Reveries 4

Anna Counts the Morning Blackbirds: six views 8

Digression: Sad Young Man on a Train 9

Packing My Sweetcase 10

Further Lovely Lettuce Lore 14

Digression: St. Patrick's Day, 2015 16

Love Song 20

What Anna Wants 22

Digression: Dreams 25

Anna's House (a dialogue in three voices) 27

*Near dusk,
a woman wanders in the garden,
tugging at scallions and brazen radishes,
breaking new greens cleanly
at the base. She recalls
the daughter of Juno and wild lettuce
rising from the cool earth. Soon,
she too will lie there.*

In the Morning, What the Light Provides:

                                     a parabolic space   the dark
                                          triangle beyond

Say: I am lying in the middle of the bed, on my
stomach. or right side. hands cuppin me face as if to save
meself. birdson(g). (bridesong) raucous: the
clockwork to the
                              UP
right and upUP a little and Up   above the bed and (where I
am always lying in the mi(u)ddle, alone) the rhododendron lea

ves wetoakleavesun. Light is.

     self: the eternal deferment

                                       :
                                     ir
                                e   ruption
                   dis
                                  inter

inneruption
/ure

           sleep

                 wake

                       break

                             noflesh
                         nopain

Immobile eye (I)
immobile eye beyond the dark beforedark   arc   the
letters'
     appearances
the(ir) birth

                 sometimes when I sit at the brown desk, the
wood becomes heavy beneath my voice; the wor(l)d becomes

      heavy benea

The dark:thewall:neither to the left nor at my feet where I
had felt it in the night how could i not know its place its
placement now dark beside me going under again for the
third
timegoing
                        down
                                      I could feel it beginning a
gain
          this life
                  form-curve-come: forward from the darkbeyond
it won't; it hasn't any point (to penetrate); nothing;
nothing stable, count
                  able; it slides in sideways, settles,
ssspins, a disc opening softly   fixed the periphery
lying
     , be-lyingwhite emptyluminous
                        arc in the curve of space
: its pure articulation and its name: the start(le) before
desire
                the small ex
                      /clamation
                             o
                             ~~~/^
)
                                    -+++
                    *[
                     !

And the waist
is it she
the small
tightened
breath
                of the leaves' wetness, the knees the dark
triangle beyond
                      window (,) always   Above and opened
slightly, the darkness beyond, someone leaning forward,

                                                    her
    herface her dark
                  ness
                        o

Anna's Reveries

if I were to write .000000000000000000000000 ad infinitum (until i die, until i died, did die), stopping only to eat, drink, sleep, defecate, urinate, and procreate (and do we stop to breathe? dunno. dunno.) in order to show the magnificent magnitude of the infinitesimal smallness (oh, tiny, tiny) and insignificance--there, i said it--of my being/being in relation to the whole entire universey, would that be any less a meaningful(l) striving than those in which i now (and forever: until i die, did die) in which i (k)now engage? how to imagine--imagine--the enormity of space...

                                      our lovely space
(s),
gaps,
wisps,
vacancies:
oh lovely lovely emptiness

of stones (*pierre, pietra, carreg*):
                        where have you come from o lovely ones? from underground we rise like swellings of love we rise we welcome you dark ones we are the white the pebbles under your tongue the prayer stones the cairns we are with you always we are the wall behind the terrace where stonecrop grows and Russian sage (how far you have traveled, *Perovskia*, from the loessial steppes) we are the granite and marble chips caressing graves

                              "if you go to Kevin Lynch's grave after 5 PM have a care."
Each evening for several hours his father is there.
have a care/the stones are there/
caressing Kevin Lynch's grave in County Derry.

                             hunger/hunger/hungry/ones
                   (a cry is a mouth beside a bird)

                    we are the sharp blue stones "where pilgrims walked barefoot [*o stones of fire*] to wound their feet" to wound, to find, to heal. we are the rift in the saddened earth

constellations counter-clockwise go: e to w
        (here a calling out is)
    earth moves clockwise: w to e
        (here in the time of the
    little world. what joys there are here,
      oh, what)
    and anna circles round and round
        (sorrows,
        here in the world
        the little sighing world)
    and round and lands and melts and is
    a small white circle on my shoe:
    mummy, mummy
        (people lie on grassy hilltops
        singing)
    a small white circle
           (*Anna, are you in there?*)
        (singing
        oh, what joys here
        oh, what sorrows bear us
        in the singing sighing world of
        broken)
    and to and fro is Anna
    circling, swirling, swaying
        (here the shattered world lies
        here the fragrant bees are

            buzzhum/buzzhum
    in the nectar's lately sorrow
    humming)
        (*Anna's Reveries): someone is humming a song for me: it
might be a song in the forest; it might be a song by the sea*
        (Here I come to call you
            (*Anna, others, are you there?*)
    but you do not answer
    singing sighing in the world of
    lasting.)

            weft is the filling thread,
            warp is the ~~~~~~~~~~

ab initio
I have loved you
      little little one(s)

        Hair under water, hair in flames, hair that d[r]ies before the
fire...

      {fly}   {fly}   {fly   away

          home}

In the dark poet silently each thing/repeats itself: a star, a house *[Anna, your house will come into the meadow 'fore mo(u)rning]*, a wood. Feather, ruby, star and onion grass will live here. And in
    the tree nearby *strouthia*/sparrows/littlebirds.

Many things are twiziters and twitters here.

                Will there be
  a tree
    beside the birds?
        Will it be
ever green
    (as we)

"It's a silly tree," you said;
    "I never should have bought it."
    Years later, it is still a silly tree
    that blossoms near my vacancy.
    Silly woman, silly tree, I love you.

This is Anna's song.
The song has
no refrain.
no refrain.
        people live in the rurals, in the urbans
          Anna lives beside them there alone.
            Anna talks to (no) one
              one/one

Anna whispers loudly/in the forest
(it might be a house in the forest,
it might be a house by the sea0

Every year when Spring was Coming, the Flower was Blooming. Today is the First Day when Spring was Coming (3/02/02). In the Garden, the Rabbit is Curly. "I am having the dizzies today," Says AnnA.

Anna Counts the Morning Blackbirds
    : 6 *views*

3. Three polyoptic cr3ws against the sky:

1. A cr1w perches on the back of the chair on the left, pecks at the green unyielding metal, the color of yews.

2. Although I have never seen cr2ws in the yews.

4. "Don't eat the cr4w, poisonous on the tongue."

5. Why is there a large cr5w photographing me as I place my small pebble in the glass jar?

11. Cr6ws hang upside down in the branches. Hunger overcomes them. Hunger: it overcomes.

Digression: Sad Young Man on a Train
   -Marcel Duchamp (1911)

1) an express carries its cargo of sleeping children thru the icy night. frigid eerie dark. solitary night.

2) squares of light. a face against the pane. barred by the dark pines. in the small town surrounding the lake, the train leaves the bridge, a colt leaping the pasture fence, then down, down into the frigid water. the murky water. straight down dark. gone.

3) and boy, was it you lowered into the well? down here. down here. bring up the bucket. raise the dead. Boy, can you hear me?

Questions for discussion: and reader, did the descent into the well disturb you too? or only the train? the train with the father disappearing inside.

Packing My Sweetcase

the curve-cry of the joy
(amouthbesideabird)
the joy-curve of the cry
(amouthbesideabird)
the cry inside the word
(amouthbesideabird)
                                        the cry's
  startled
            o
                    (in Anna's House there lives a mouth beside a bird a cry
  inside the word the mouth's startled *o* in Anna's House)

cry is a mouth beside a bird
 woods is two trees standing side by side

   desiresubjectotherobjectriskperishrapturerupturedeath
                                        ravish
                    ravish
ravish

"Whatsoever is an arising thing that also is a ceasing thing?"

  and you to whom I address my words
 (you who like to enjoy me)

          ☠✞☼✌
          ☠✞☼✌
          ☠✞☼✌

✋ ♎□ ■□◆ &■□⬩ ⍓□◆ ⍓♏◆📪 ✋ ♒♏♋❒
⍓□◆❒ ♍❒⍓ ⬩♒□ ♋❒♏ ⍓□◆⬧✍ ☠◆❒♋✍
          it'sveryclearlythislovethatIgifttoyoulongablelongablelove
                                        : *cuerpo de mujer, blanc as colinas,*
muslos blancos/body of a woman, white hills, white thighs
                                                            melos, melos:
                                                  melisma
                                                      melissa
                                                  melisma
                                                      melissa
                                                                      soughsoughsoft

susurrant/soo(the)soo(the)whisperrustlemurmur

"To have a home,
a little house in a green garden,
stillness everywhere"
                    :this wee myselfie here with you
                          you
                                  N(ura)
                                                          (a bird with wings)
                          ku ku
                      (where? where?)

.her name is Appolonia.
                                              .her name is *onoma*.

my pure (Ozark honey) bee:
blackberry
wild sweet clover
(let me drink your wild thyme)
persimmons
water willow
wild mint
wild fruit trees--
plum, cherry, peach

                    "bee"boatshoneyboatsfloatingboats: wu
                                shr
                    ohlifeisasailinghouseisaport

to broke the space,
        I
                the milk was about to consume the day the
                              night milk
                                  mother
                                      jar

            -ring ringing: let me pack you in my sweetcase night-mother
milkmaid

                    when the garden was
established profoundly,

almost they walked hurriedly
to get there: to the sailing,
to the little port; firstable,
upon arriving, "the bee
is blue," she said,
and "how did you

pass the night?"
she said:
Boganda
Luganda
Kuganda: "How did you
            How did you
            Pass the night?"

I'm walkin' with my sweetca(u)se on the wild, wide-shouldered shores
of love

              :my blue windflower-
ing sweet little light
(ness)
  sleeping or not
  a white plate or blue
  blue dusk or dark
(ness)
  what we find
what we don't
 what we lose
 what we keep
  one, two, one two:
  Ek, Do, Ek, Do
     either/or/and/or

           Here is a tiny house
            with no one inside it.

                Anna, are you in there?
                            Anna?

        Anna Altheia, the unconcealed one.

(Miss Mousie, please
unmarry me)
                Here is a ladder ☒ with no one to climb
   (It gives me the quivers and swillies to tell you about it.

         "Spoons of the Wee," the forks and knives lie restless in
the pantry in the kitchen drawer)

                        :from her fingertips humming

Further Lovely Lettuce Lore
(from (A)nna (M)orphous: days)

1) Venus held the lovely Phaon responsible for Sappho's death, and turned him into a lettuce.

2) Aristoxemus sprinkled the lettuces in his garden with wine and honey and picked them the next day at dawn; "green cakes," he called them, that had been given to him by the earth.

3) It is rumored that Venus slept on a bed of soothing lettuce to forget Adonis.

4) Deer are needed to eat the insects that spread bacteria to lettuce plants.

…hushaby, my lovely … *laitue, lechuga, lattuca, Lattich*: Riccia Rossa d'America, Rosso di Trento, Freckles/Trout Back, Bibb, Black Seeded Simpson, Green Ice, St. Blaise, Summertime, Red Grenoble, Tango, Red Sails (tum de dum), Reines des Glaces, North Pole…

                        anemone, my wild blue
                              flower
                      /ing lettuce *a Chroidha dhil*

    who are suffer
    hungry?
    not I
    not I
            [but wasn't the mother was? is?]

                Oh the days of the Kerry dancers
                Oh the ring of the piper's tune

Rrougette du Midi, Winter Density, Rouge d' Hiver, Winter Marvel, Selma-Wisa, Bronze Mingnonette, Tom Thumb, Red Rebosa, Lovina (oh my lovely), Deertongue, Apollo, Buttercrunch, Sierra, Croquerelle du Midi, Esmeralda, Red Riding Hood…

    andonedayinautumn,thedarkshadows

All the days of my life, "You know can happen something, but you not know what's happen."

...Rosalita, Arctic Kind, Brune d' Hiver, Rossimo, Brunia, Olga, *oh* Valeria....

Digression in Five Parts: St. Patrick's Day 2015

1.

Having earlier quaffed the quoof in County Armagh,
the family of Paul Muldoon
(in Uncle Pat's Ford, on Sundays)
motored from graveyard to graveyard
repeating the names on the cold stones:

        Duffy
        MacGinnis
        Muldoon
        Malone

        (whisper)

until one day they discovered a new digression,
the roundabout in Balleygawley:
now round and round they circled and sang--

                          Duffy
                          MacGinnis
                          Muldoon
Ballygoroundgogolly: Malone--

        (shout)

renaming the cycle of birth and death: their words behind them light as
air:
Absolute. Weightless. Real.
D
M
M
M
  -duffymacginnismuldoonmalone

2.

fuzees
jarvey

jellybags
huxter

harts tongue
woolly bobs
boreen pinkeens
whortleberries
and Lucan Looks Lovely
at Waxtries Glen

:and on the hill those beasts that have long inseminated the imagination
of our protoplasts

(surely, we were there
at darkfall; surely, we were holding
space and air)
      Armagh
      Muldoon
      McGinnis
      Malone

3.

Rooting Day/Leaving Dublin/August Twenty-sixth

walk lawn gardenwildgarden(s): gardens chaotic beyond
containment.
   when her gardens moved outward outward (s) out
beyondhernolonger
contained, Fidelma tangled fuchsia in her goldilocks o. In
Dublis'faircityo, D4 and D5,
  she
looks for a garden small and.
      In twenty-seven years, I have never let my
gardens
go-how does your garden how--to this extent
     sic transit gloria mundi. Never.

     housethorn
    house thorn

desire   's a garden in riotous bloom   or
desire: a garden in riotous bloom   or   she
desires   a garden in riotous bloom or

                                          mood gorning
                                          serry munshine
                                                  mudshine

                  it's a lovely walk he said alovelyday:

4.

        Iggy's Irish Laws

    1) You can't win.
    2) !@~#$^&*)_+j You can't even break even.
    3) You can't get out of the game.

            Fidelma's Three Laws of Anti-Absolutism

        1) Nothing is what it seems,
        2) but we have to call things by name
anyway,
        3) but not so seriously, please.

3) dreaming
3) dreaming a treatise on knees:
                      A knee is weeping as I write,
etc.

            Linden's Laws of Deconstructionist Theory

1) You may say skive off any workshop you wish;
    2) any word may be made up to constitute a meaning
        (see fic
3) You need to lie in bed and think this over for several hours/days

        (Mooney and Muldooney sitting in a tree
                                      /w-r-i-t-i-n-g

                                                                     hee
                                                                      hee
                                                                     hee

By Golly By Gawley
the world continues round
and(a)roundand(a)roundand(a)round

Black and black is the Irish Sea.

Love Song

I think that I shall call you too *elision*, the darkness into the little away: sweet Annie, elision, Ameria, amor--*Apis mellifera*--my sweet be(e). Slipping away into the little darkness and almost the day over left so little there, the slipping away, and *o*(h) the every exists/ "In itself," Karl says, "every existence appears round."

        And here, let us beginning again we; here, in the Temple of Accumulated Frag-ments: *ici/ici/ici*

    Jack speaks of the trivium of grammar,
       logic,
          rhetoric;
I speak
the trillium
of love

      tra la
      the trillium
  of love
       ~~~*tra la la tweedly dee dee it gives me a thrill--to wake up in the morning on the* trillium *hill*

but The wor(l)d is gone now I have to carry you

oh, the weary, the word-gone-weary world
memory, memory, desire, memory, desire, signs, memory, desire, signs, thin, memory, desire, thin, trading, desire, signs, thin, trading, eyes, signs, thin, trading, eyes, names, thin, trading, eyes, names, dead, trading, eyes, names, dead, sky, eyes, names, dead, sky, continuous, names, dead, sky, continuous, hidden, dead, sky, continuous, hidden, sky, continuous, hidden continuous, hidden, hidden she is she is:

Diomira,
Isidora,
Dorothea,
Jaira,
Anastasia,
Tamara,
Zora,
Despina,

Valdrada,
Olivia
(my Sweet O(b)livia Armeria Amour),

Sophronia,
Eutropia,
Zemrude,
Aglurea,
Octavia,
Ersilia,
Baucis,
Leandra,
Melania,
Esmerelda
(O Esmerelda Soybean, the third sweet daughter) and on and on it goes
                                                     ~~and (the) women
    invisible all
                                                             andhereicom
ereadyornotunearthingyouearthstarhereontherice-grainhollowhallowedhillo
nthelovelylovelytrillium-hallowed hill, my sweet,
   my *elision* bee

What Anna Wants

what does woman want?

AnnaAnnaAnnaAnnaAnnaAnnaAnnaAnna☞ ⑤⑤♋AnnaAnnaAnna❦■
■♋❦■■♋Anna
Anna❦■■♋❦■■♋❦■■♋💻

"I am having the dizzies today,"

                                                          says Anna.

"It would seem that every detail concerning the crystallography of ice and snow should have been known long ago, but our knowledge of crystalline water is not yet perfect."

        "And they are coming to visit today," says Anna: THE SNOWFLAKE'S CLOSEST OF KIN, AND ITS COUSIN, THE DEWDROP;
also also:
ice flowers
windowpane frost
rime
glaze
sleet
graupel

        and An[n]a and friends
   to sleep with, my body and poetry.

"First you catch your snow crystal." But it is nothing, mummy, almost nothing. Where are they, and where am I going? And when we disappear, and the little darkness settles all around?
(and we/the vanishing we(e)/we too/two/are almost no/thing/too)

                            Polynya, she
lives
by the ocean, *Polynya*
she lives
by the sea   (she is a Russian Princess, after all)

Polyonymous
lying in the snows is*
hushes hushes

we all lie down.

"But it is so tiny, so fragile, and so evanescent save in the coldest of weather, that few, very few indeed, have come to know the snow crystal at first hand." But she is so tiny, so fragile.... Very few have come to know my Anna at first hand. At first touch. Most will never know her/she/we/I is*AnnaAnnaAnna,*
for *"I is another,"* says Anna.

* Pretzel, Feather, Pause, Lament, Clowning:

> *here are*
> > Many Meaning Objects:
> > > FooFoo and PimPim
> > > > bright scarves and cinnamon
> > > > > a woman writing in the evening dark
> > > > > > lying in the snows is
> > > > > > > hid(e) behind our eyes is.

joyance/joi/Joyceful(l)/joyful/*jouissance*/joyance/joi/Joyceful(l)/*jouissance*/ joyance/joi/Joyceful(l)/j: all are little J-pegs to hang our sorrow on: williwaws, black flaws, the winds blow hard today.

This is the shoe that fits you; wear it. This is the hand that bites you; feed it. This is the world askew (hush, baby, the world will hear you) thisisthepotthatboilswatchitthisistheblueskydarkening: sometimes my heart, it brokens:
"Mother carry me, I too will carry you."

here we go Heidy, ho!
here we go Heidy, o(h)!

> "We *all* have the dizzies today,"
> sings Anna.

> > > I fell into the sleep;
> > > > I slipped and slid there longly;
> > > > > I heard their voices calling:
> > > > > > *Anna Polyonymous*

> *Polysemous Anna,*
carry on your shadows' wings my sorrow

Anna, are you in there? Anna, *can you hear me?*

No one and no thing, remember, is more than a slight perturbation in space. Neither you nor I.

Here is a bowl of words for you,

Anna Diachronous,
delicious words for
Anna M:
Miss Mnemosyne,
My darling,
Ms. mnenon,
the *Rememberer:*

        but "Where have all the words for memory gone?

~~mouth
~~~mother
    ~~~~~mothwings:

((((let us forget her: Lemosyne, your fateful twin))))

    --and all remembered spaces we have love(d)

Digression: Dreams
    -Akira Kurosawa (1990)

disappear
        -ed
                -ing
just turned a
        round I/
                the man in Kurosawa's film
walked into Van Gogh
's
        painting, past

the frame
        into a field of sun
-flowers

      just turn
-ed around
        as a wave
                black wave

in an imaginary movie "in the style of
        Polanski's *Gunter Kine*rt"

                gone I
just
      a wave washes
over a man's house and family and
they disappear
                + "The earth is still sprinkled

                      [sprinklesprink]
                [williewinklewe]
[w/] flowers, only now it is empty"

            sunflower
woods
        goneagaingone

                                I
                                                just turned around and

                                a small man walks into a field of
sunflowers
                    +

                        then he walks on and on and
                                                        gone, he
                                                        gone
brief (ly)
            whisk
                        wisp
                            (w)hisp
-er

around + just
                        they
                                (dis)appear(ing).

Anna's House
(a dialogue in three voices)

2nd voice
(the mediator)

                    it might be a House in a forest
                        it might be a House by the sea

~ ~ ~ ~ ~ ~ ~ ~ ~
~ ~ ~ ~ ~ ~ ~ ~

      3rd voice
(the anna)

someone (*I*) is (*want*) building (*to*) a (*be*) house (*a*) for (*person*) me (*like*) a (*someone*) pure (*else*) white (*was*) house (*once*). . . . It might be a house in a meadow; it might be a house on a hill (see there on the hill how someone gathers pollen; barely a w(h)isp(er), she makes no cry). the pine trees wait on the hill nearby. soon, this too will come to pass--this day and that--and grasses fold their tiny blades and sleep

2nd voice
(the mediator)

in anna's House there lives a mouth beside a bird a cry/inside the word the mouth's/startled o in anna's House

3rd voice
(the anna)

and in my house there will be a small window
there will the light be
and the empty spaces/there
      with you beside there
on the rice grain hill my frangible mirrored/self
of the self
        o how your voice rings out
    of the hollow
 -ness there
        you

4th voice
(the innominate one)

does it exist?
1st voice
(the questioner)

Where is the ladder that climbs to the sky?

3rd voice
(the anna)

                    :hellofarewellhello:

Someoneiscomingnearer
someoneisbuildingahouseforme: itmightbe
a *House*   a *House*
inside the house
there will be a shadow

Someone is coming nearer
                                now she gently permeates
        her
    I hear ^ footsteps approaching

the house will be in a meadow
the house will be by the sea

2nd voice
(the mediator)

inside the house there will be
1) a fennel bloom
2) a circumpolar bluet
(Enallagma cyanigerum)
Narrow-winged damselfly

1st voice
(the questioner)

Inside the house will there will there be

3) a small giraffe (the giraffe is invisible) enfolding Anna's metamorphosis in her wings?

(in 1944, Virginia Woolf's Asheham house in the Sussex downs was destroyed by the east Sussex county council. it was destroyed "to make way for a rubbish dump.")

2nd voice
(the mediator)

we must be v. careful, anna Armeria sweet oblivia amour, that once yr. house is built, it is never so destroyed. never destroyed. no, never.

3rd voice
(the anna)

        someone is weeping
          the floor for us
            in the interstices of our house
                :such weeping with
the long-handled bloom: swish and whoosh, hush and wish…

2nd voice
(the mediator)

her name is *appolonia*
her name is *onoma*

3rd voice
(the anna)

this wee myselfie here with you

1st voice
(the questioner)

What does Anna think about while she peels potatoes?
While she peas the shells and kisses the mouth beside the bird?
Will the bird swallow Anna?
Will Anna swallow the mouse?
Will the swallow mouse the bird?

When will the bird fly away?
When will the mouth fly away?
Will Anna ever leave the blue dark nest?
What does the mouth say to Anna?

**3rd voice
(the mediator)**

"*O(h),*" says the mouth to anna: "*oh.*"

        (AnnaBlossom! Anna, A-N-N-A, I trickle thy name.

              . . . most glorious of all, thou art from the back, / as from the front:
A-N-N-A)

**3rd voice
(the anna)**

Every years when Spring was Coming, the Flower was Blooming. Today is the First Day when Spring was Coming (3/21/02). In the Garden, the Rabbit is Curly.

"I am having the dizzies today,"

**2nd voice
(the mediator)**

says anna.

Notes

"Anna's Reveries"

"If you go to Kevin…," Ed Wandall, *The Irish American*, Vol. III, No. 1, Oct. 2002, 14-15. Kevin Lynch was the last of the young men to die during the hunger strikes in Northern Ireland.

"cry is a mouth beside a bird, woods is two trees standing side by side" are Chinese ideograms from Greg Winechup's *The Heart of Chinese Poetry*.

"where pilgrims walked…," Edna O'Brien, *James Joyce* (Penguin Lives).

"Hair under water…," Louise Bourgeois diary entry.

"In the dark poet…," Rainer Marie Rilke

"Packing My Sweetcase"

the words *curve, cry, joy* are a play on a phrase from Valdimir Nabokov's *ADA*: "the joy-cry of the curve."

"Whatsoever is an arising thing…," is from Nura Petrov's *Dalhousie Journal*.

cuerpo de mujer….," ("Body of Woman") is a poem by Pablo Neruda.

"To have a home…," is from Herman Hesse's *Wandering*.

"Spoons of the Wee" is from John McPhee's *The Crofter and the Laird*.

"Further Lovely Lettuce Lore"

Food facts are from Maguelonne Toussaint-Samat's *History of Food*. (Trans. Anthea Bell).

The names of various lettuces are from spring seed catalogues.

"You know something can happen…," Christo, lecture at Lafayette College, Easton, PA, 1999.

"Digression: St. Patrick's Day, 2015"

"Irish Laws" composed by poets Ignatius McGovern, Dublin, Ireland; Fidelma Gallagher, Dublin, Ireland; and Linden Ontje, Los Angeles, CA and Alaska, USA (at The Poets House, Islandmagee, Northern Ireland, 1994).

"fuzees, jarvey," etc. are from Austin Clark's *Twice Round the Black Church*.

"Love Song"

"In itself…," Karl Jaspers

The "trivium of grammar…," Jacques Derrida.

"memory, memory, desire…," and the names of cities ("Diomira, Isidora, Dorothea…,") are from Italo Calvino's *Invisible Cities*.

"What Anna Wants"

"What does woman want?" is the famous question from the tongue of the brilliant misogynist, Freud. All words in this poem in Comic Sans MS/Italics are Freud's.

References and quotes re snow and crystallography are from W. A. Bentley and W. J. Humphreys' *Snow Crystals*.

"and An[]na and friends…," Tomaz Salamun

Polynya is an area of open water in an ice sea.

"Pretzel, Feather…," is from Walter Benjamin's "Thought Figures" in *Selected Writings*.

Foo Foo and Pim Pim were the imaginary friends of my granddaughter, Kenza.

"Anna's House"

"*I want to be a person like someone else once…,*" is from Peter Handle's (Trans. Michael Rollof) *Kasper and other Plays.*

"A-N-N-A, I trickle thy name…," is from Kurt Schwitters "Anna Blossom Has Wheels," *Merz Poem No. 1.*

Julie Cooper-Fratrik received her MFA from Goddard/VT College. She is a former Bucks County Poet Laureate (PA) and the winner of the first Robert Fraser Award from Bucks County Community College, where she was on the language and literature faculty for 23 years. She is the author of two poetry collections, *The Slow Separations* and *Breathing Lesons (a remembering)*; and is Co-editor, with Chris Bursk, of "A Gathering of Voices: Survivors and Friends Speak Out Against Domestic Violence" (James A. Michener Art Museum and A Woman's Place). Chapters from her prose work, "Beyond the Objects of Desire: The Space of the Poet in the Space of the World," has been published in *Under the Sun* and *Tupelo Quarterly*. She has published poetry in, among others, *The Dickinson Review, Quarter After Eight, Hayden's Ferry Review, Ekphrasis, Slant, Natural Bridge,* and *the mssissippi review*. She lives in rural Pennsylvania between Philadelphia and New York City, where she and her spouse plant organic gardens, make art, discuss ideas, and generally enjoy life.

www.ingramcontent.com/pod-product-compliance
Lightning Source LLC
LaVergne TN
LVHW041554070426
835507LV00011B/1083